ALL THINGS GIRL

Girls Rock!

TERESA TOMEO
MOLLY MILLER
MONICA COPS

The "All Things Girl" series is published by
Bezalel Books
Waterford, MI
www.BezalelBooks.com

The titles in the ALL THINGS GIRL series are:

Friends, Boys, and Getting Along

Mirror, Mirror on the Wall…What is Beauty After All?

Girls Rock!

Mind Your Manners

Modern and Modest

All Things Girl Journal

References to the Catechism of the Catholic Church are denoted: CCC

ISBN 978-0-9818854-3-8
Library of Congress Control Number 2008931735

To Teresa Tomeo, Cheryl Dickow, thank you all your work on this book series and for giving me the opportunity to use my "feminine genius." To Monica Cops, my "Ethel" and dear friend, and to women I have known and loved over the years who have used their gifts to further the Faith: Lisa McDermott, Laureen Davey, Terri Muskevitch, Brenda Ketter, Pamela Hamman, Julie Christian, Kathy Ellenbecker, Heather Hruby, Suzanne Ellis, Cindy Quick, and Jynel Brockhaus. I love you all.
Rock On Ladies, Rock On!
Molly

To all my nieces: Anne, Mary, Sarah, Catherine, Meghan, Clare and MariJose; You rock!
Love, Aunt (Tia) Monica

To all the young girls, remember you can do all things in Christ who strengthens you. Now go rock the world and make a difference!
Teresa Tomeo

Table of Contents

High class ... 5

Feminine Genius ... 7

Take it from Teresa ... 13

Vocations ... 17

Great Women ... 24

Feminism vs. Femininity ... 34

Celebrate Being a Girl ... 36

Virtues to Live by ... 42

You've Gotta Have a Plan ... 46

A Girl Like Me ... 49

High Class

All people begin life in their mother's womb. From the beginning of your creation, tiny as you were, you were a person. Being created a person, and not, let's say, a kitty or a dog, is special because God gave you a soul that will live forever. A person is a creature made up of a body and a soul. As a person, you are in a "higher class" because your soul is what gives you "the image and likeness of God". Your Creator, God the Father has stamped on your soul, dignity. What is dignity? It is your worth as a person.

Dignity has three characteristics:

1) You have it no matter what circumstances you live in.

2) You have it no matter what you look like.

3) You have it, no matter what changes you go through in your life.

Here are some examples of dignity...

Jennifer lives in a neighborhood where the houses are very small and the people work hard but don't have much money. Katie lives in a mansion and takes expensive vacations every year. *Which person has more dignity?*

Jade is from Africa and has deep brown skin. Julie has red hair and freckles. Laura is chubby. Maggie is tall and skinny. *Which girl has more dignity?*

Opal is 95 years old and lives in a nursing home and has to be spoon fed. Riley was in a car accident and has a huge scar on her face. Jessica is a beautiful movie star. *Which person has more dignity?*

Hopefully you answered "neither" to all of the examples because all people are equal in dignity. You will go through good and bad times, happiness and sadness, success and failure in your life. Sometimes people think these things are what define you. This is a lie you must not believe.

At this point you should be feeling pretty good about yourself.

Just in case you need more, check it out, it gets better!

Always remember that your dignity is
a precious gift from God!

The Feminine Genius

In 1995 Pope John Paul II wrote a special letter to women. He wanted you, and all the women of the world, to know that you are quite special. He also wanted to thank all women just for being female and for using their God-given gifts. Wow!!! That's pretty cool: the Pope writing a letter just for you!

The Holy Father uses a description for women called "the feminine genius." What is that? Simply put, the feminine genius is the gift women have to give of themselves freely and with love. This includes all women: single, wives, mothers, daughters, sisters, workingwomen, and consecrated women (nuns and sisters). John Paul realized just how much women throughout history have contributed in family life, to society, and culture. He understood that when women listened to God and loved Christ they were very powerful! All they had to do was be themselves! Imagine how wonderful that is…

just be who God made you to be and you will be powerful, indeed.

Let's go back. When Adam and Eve sinned, woman's dignity went down the drain because men began to dominate women. This was **not** what God intended. He created them equal. Different, but equal. You see, before original sin, Eve, woman, wanted to give herself freely. She wanted to care for Adam, the animals, and the garden. Sin ruined this, just like it ruins everything. Once sin entered the world, Eve was forced to give and work, like a servant or a slave. Not out of love like the original plan.

However, because God loved us so much, He fixed this situation in Mary, Our Blessed Mother. As the mother of Jesus, she became the "new Eve," that is, she restored the dignity of women that was lost by sin. Mary gave her Son, out of love, for the world. Mary showed us what God had originally intended when He made us. She was able to say "yes" to what God was asking and became a role model of how we all can say "yes" to God.

Mary represents all women. Since then, women are liberated!

What Did Jesus Think?

Being a girl is special. You know that, and Jesus did, too. When He was alive on Earth, women and girls did not have as many opportunities as they do today. Jesus didn't care what others thought; He believed women had dignity, (personal worth) and He showed it. Remember the story in the Bible when he met a woman at the well? She was forced to go to the well late in the afternoon when it was super hot because she was an outcast. This woman had committed a lot of serious sins and was living with a man who was not her husband. Jesus did not hold her sin against her but began talking to her. This was way amazing! Jesus was making sure everyone understood that personal worth is not something that can be removed or erased or reduced in a person. Jesus was saying to that woman, so that we all could understand, that no matter what, He loved her (and me and you). Can you even imagine how she must have felt? She must have been overwhelmed by Jesus' love just like any of us will be overwhelmed by His love when we really understand that it is there for us no matter what!

Think about the lady with the hemorrhage. Have you ever read her story? She had so much faith in Jesus she thought that just by touching the hem of his clothes she would be healed of her lifelong problem. What did Jesus do? He healed her and publicly pointed out her great faith.

Then there's the adulterous women who was about to be stoned. Jesus didn't condemn her but had compassion towards her. He forgave her for her sins. Why? Because His love for her (and me and you) is greater than any sin we may have committed. Women are so special Jesus did not want them to think any less of themselves because of sin. He knew He would die for all these women and wanted the world to remember how precious they were in His eyes.

Who can forget the women at the cross? Our Blessed Mother and Mary Magdalene are the ones we recognize. While most of the disciples ran away, the women were brave and loyal to the very end. Jesus rewarded Mary Magdalene by appearing to her after His resurrection. Not only did Jesus reward her but He must have counted on her, just like He counts on you! Jesus knew women would help Him carry out His Father's plans. Jesus is counting on you, too, to make the world an amazing place. Remember, that's why John Paul II said *you have power*!

You are a precious gem to Jesus!

You Need to Know!

Sometimes, our Catholic Church has been accused of repressing women through history. You need to know as a young Catholic girl that this is a lie! As you grow up it is important for you to know the truth of the Catholic Church teachings.

Check out the facts below.
This is your heritage as a Catholic and as a girl!

- The Catholic Church is called "The bride of Christ" and is always referred to with a feminine pronoun.
- The Catholic Church has taught from its very beginning that women have a special dignity. Women are meant to form part of and be active in a living and working society.
- The Catholic Church fought to change laws to make sure women were not taken advantage of.
- Only the Catholic Church influenced cultures to allow women choices in their lives such as whether to marry or not.
- It was the Church who encouraged women's endeavors such as establishing schools, hospitals, convents, and other charitable works for the poor.

THE CATHOLIC CHURCH HAS ALWAYS TAUGHT…

- Women should never "masculinize" themselves, that is, make themselves like men. Instead, they should embrace their feminine gifts.
- If women try to be like men, they will not only end up unhappy, they will never be who they are meant to be.
- The personal traits of women are different than those of men.

THE FACTS ARE…

- Women who used their feminine gifts to the full have accomplished great works through history," as much as men and, more often than not they did so in much more difficult conditions." (John Paul's Letter to Women)
- Women's influence in history has shaped the lives of many generations, right up to yours.
- Even now, women continue to be valued more for their physical appearance than for their skill, their talents, and their intellectual abilities. Isn't that sad?
- Women see people with their hearts and always want to help others.
- "The Blessed Mother is the highest expression of "the feminine genius," (John Paul's letter to Women), and she is a source of constant inspiration.

Princess

When you were a baby, your mom and dad brought you to church to be baptized. What does baptism do? It washes away original sin, makes you a child of God and fills your soul with grace. God is the King of the universe, and you are His daughter: that makes you a princess! As a princess in the royal family of God, you have a value greater than a rare jewel and He loves you soooooo much. This is what defines you as a person and nothing, including popularity, good grades, designer clothes or money, makes a difference in who you are in the sight of God your Father.

So you see, you are so much more than body parts. You are intelligent, creative and caring. You are not an object, but a person, and a female person at that! Sexuality is what makes you a girl, different from males. Only a woman can carry another living person within her body. God also gave to women unique gifts such as a nurturing heart, a giving spirit, and a detail oriented mind. These gifts are used for the good of those around you and for your own true happiness.

Lots of girls grow up trying to answer the soul searching question of *"Why am I here?"*

The answer is simple; *To know, love, and serve God in this life and to be happy with Him forever in Heaven in the next.*

You get to *know, love and serve God from Jesus Christ, the Son of God, who teaches us through the Catholic Church.*

But how do you do all these? Let's go step by step:

1. To know God:

What would you do if you want to get to know a movie star? You'd try to read up all the information about him or her in magazines and books, you would watch interviews on T.V., ask people around you what they know, etc. Well, you get to know God in a similar way: reading the Bible, listening to your parents talk about God, listening in religion class seriously, praying and receiving the Sacraments.

2. To love God:

Did you ever notice that when you have a really good friend you want to spend more and more time with her? And then, the more time you spend with her the more you love her? It's the same way with God. To love God, you need to spend time with Him in prayer, adoring and thanking Him for your blessings, and worshipping Him at Sunday Mass. The amazing thing is, just like with a good friend, the more time you spend with God the more you will love Him!

3. To Serve God:

You serve God by serving other people. Serving God is doing daily chores cheerfully without complaining. You serve God when you serve other people through your kind words and compassionate ways. You serve God when you participate in community service projects or do things like visit residents in a nursing home. God is in each and every person so when you serve other people, you are serving God!

As you grow up,
ask Our Lord in what special way
He wants you to know, love and serve Him.
This will be your vocation
and will make you truly happy in your life.

Girls Rock! We do indeed. We know this because God tells us so. He made us in His image and likeness and from the beginning of the human race with Adam and Eve we were special. Through the Bible, God's word, we also can see that girls rock and that we have a major role to play in the Kingdom of Christ and His plan of salvation. It starts out in the very first book of the Old Testament which says...

"And I will put enmity between you and the woman and between your offspring and hers; He will crush your head and you will strike his heel."

It was our Blessed Mother's "yes" that we read about in the first chapter of St. Luke's Gospel that allows for Jesus to come into this world and walk and live among us. She said...

"I am the handmaid of the Lord. Let it be done to me according to thy word."

Other women who lived in Jesus' time also were given important roles to play in God's plan because Jesus treated women with dignity and made them part of His ministry. St. Mary Magdalene, a close friend of our Lord's, was given the amazing privilege of being the first to see the resurrected Lord on that first Easter Sunday Morning. It was Mary Magdalene who was sent to tell St. Peter and the other apostles about the risen Christ.

The many great Catholic saints who have gone before us also remind us that girls do indeed rock. Just like St. Paul tells us in Philippians 4:13

"I can do all things in Christ who strengthens me."

So what type of things do you think Jesus is calling you to do and what would you like to do when you grow up? We can be Moms. We can work outside the home and have a family or we can enter the religious life. The possibilities are endless because Jesus loves us. Remember that you are a daughter of the King and the King wants you to have an abundant life.

Sometimes when we watch TV or see a movie or read magazine, we may notice that girls are made to be objects or that they are being valued only for what they wear or look like, instead of what is in their hearts. Also, the media sometimes may try to give the world the wrong impression that girls have to act a certain way in order to be popular or accepted. Just look at what happened with pop star Jordin Sparks. The singing sensation is  determined to live a chaste life and yet she was mocked on national television for her decision to wear a purity ring. But that didn't stop her from doing the right thing. And it's a reminder that girls rock when they stand up for themselves and for who they are as precious daughters of Christ.

The media may also try to convince you that the Church is oppressive to women or that the only way girls can rock is by giving up marriage or family. But just look at some of the great women saints that went before us. Did you know that a saint who was just canonized in the last few years by the late John Paul II was not only a wife and mother who loved to spend time with her family, but she was also a doctor? St Gianna Beretta Molla was a pediatrician. She considered her work her way to serve God and to help heal people both physically and spiritually. St Gianna gave her life for her fourth child. When she learned her pregnancy would be possibly life-threatening she told her husband Pietro that if he had to choose between saving her or the baby, he should save their baby's life. Read more about this heroic woman of God in "A Girl Like Me."

Another great example for girls was the great St. Catherine of Siena, the patron saint of Italy. St. Catherine died when she was a young woman at only 33 years of age but she played a significant role in bringing the Papacy back to Rome and she also helped to establish peace among the many cities in her country that were torn apart by war. It was St. Catherine who said "when we are who we are called to be, we will set the world ablaze."

So who are you called to be? Pray and mediate upon that and ask God to show you His will for your life. What talents and interests do you have? These are

gifts from God. He would like you to use them for His glory and for His kingdom. Discerning (praying and asking God for guidance) is the perfect place to see where God may be leading you. Don't look to the media or television or Hollywood for answers. Your answers are in following God and saying "yes" just like the Blessed Mother did. Our gifts or talents are given to us by God so we can give back and make a difference and it's never too early to start praying for guidance.

So go ahead, girls. Go rock the world and be not afraid to set it ablaze for Jesus and the Church!

You're Invited!

"You therefore are to be perfect, even as your heavenly Father is perfect."

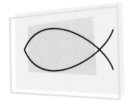

Remember these words of Our Lord to his disciples? Well, these words are for all people including you! Jesus' invitation to be perfect, to be holy, is meant to be achieved by doing everything including, schoolwork, family activities, chores out of love for God. Sound impossible? Before you get too overwhelmed, what does it actually mean to be holy? Here are a few ways to be holy:

- *Doing God's will at every moment*
- *Obeying those little "urges" to do good*
- *Realizing God is with you in everything, even small things that seem insignificant*

Jesus is the perfect model of holiness. The Blessed Mother and the saints are also models of holiness that are good to imitate. But how? There are several means to grow in holiness in your ordinary activities. Here are some of them:

1. **Follow the Commandments of God and of the Church.**
2. **Have a plan for your spiritual life such as the one at the back of this book, which includes daily prayer, devotion to Jesus in the Eucharist, frequent confession, daily examination of conscience and devotion to Our Lady.**
3. **Imitate Jesus in your daily life by doing little things out of love for Him. There are so many opportunities to do this, such as:**

    - **Reverence Jesus in the tabernacle by genuflecting, keeping a good posture during Mass and avoid getting distracted.**
    - **At school, offer up your tiredness and boredom, take good care of your school supplies, and be compassionate to other kids in the classroom.**
    - **In dealing with other people, be a good listener, learn to control your temper, avoid nasty comments, smile when you don't feel like it, and give good example to others in manners, dress and speech.**

Remember, everyone is invited to holiness. The time is NOW! The longer you wait, the harder it is. RSVP "yes" to Jesus. You'll be glad you accepted the invitation.

Vocations

Ok, you've decided to work on holiness. You're going to start a plan of life and try to do the things listed above. But, what about later, when you're an adult? What do you do then to become holy, to become a saint? Well, throughout your life, you and your parents should be praying about your vocation. "What?" you ask. You thought only nuns and priests had a vocation? Not so, dearie, not so.

A vocation is a calling from God.

It's not merely a career choice. Everyone, everyone, everyone has a calling from God!!! The word vocation refers to three different things:

1. **Vocation comes with baptism. It is a call to know, love and serve God in your life. All Christians have this vocation.**
2. **Vocation also means "state in life." This is a very broad meaning and it refers to your lifestyle such as the clergy, consecrated life, marriage or single.**
3. **Vocation means a personal relationship you have with Jesus. It is you, yourself, trying to know, love and serve God in your life.**

Now that you have an idea of all the ways the word vocation is used, you don't have to be nervous or worried if someone asks you if you have a vocation.

Everyone has to discern what it is that God has planned for them. Discern means that you pray and ask God to show you what it is He wants for you. Pope John Paul II explained in a paper he wrote that was called "On the Vocation of the Lay Faithful," that it is a "gradual process…one that happens day by day." Discerning a vocation is very different than planning a career. You see, when a person plans to be a doctor, engineer, or teacher they are thinking about what will "I" enjoy? What will make "Me" happy? What can I do for "Me" that will give "Me" satisfaction?

When a person discerns a vocation, he or she asks: **What does GOD want from me? What will make GOD happy? What would GOD like to see me do?** That's a huge difference isn't it? Guess what? When you discern, and you do what you think God wants, you **will** be happy, you **will** enjoy it and you **will** be satisfied. The key word is "will" and it is God's "will" that makes the difference! That's actually really exciting, when you think about it. So, instead of planning your future, discern your future!

There are several vocations, that is, states in life, for women: marriage, consecrated life, or single. That doesn't mean all will go perfectly or you won't encounter bad times, but you will know peace and joy through using your gifts the way God intended. Check out the descriptions below on the vocations for women. Start praying and ask Jesus to help you to see your vocation more clearly.

Marriage

If you are called to be a wife, your vocation will be to the sacrament of Matrimony. There is more to marriage than riding off into the sunset with Prince Charming. First of all, in order to receive this sacrament, you must be in the state of grace. This means one must be free from serious (mortal) sin.

The husband and wife are to comfort and support each other and they are to be faithful to each other. The purpose of marriage is to have children, raise them in the Faith, and to grow in unity with your spouse.

If marriage is your calling, it is important that you marry a Catholic. Though it is not forbidden, a "mixed marriage" is discouraged because having different beliefs is difficult in a home and within a family. Remember, a non-Catholic spouse must agree that any children born to the couple must be raised Catholic. Can you imagine trying to do that by yourself? Wow! That's a huge responsibility to take on all by yourself.

Couples who feel called to marry should pray that God direct their choice. They should also ask for guidance from their parents and parish priest. It would also be good if they receive the sacraments like confession and Communion often. One can better see the character of a person at Mass and with family. There's an old saying, "Choose your partner at the Communion rail." Makes sense, huh? Before marriage, the couple is to remain pure. This can be difficult in this day and age if both the man and the woman aren't in agreement. It involves an understanding of why God asks that of you and a respect for your Faith and your "intended."

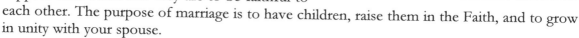

God himself is the author of marriage.
CCC #1603

*D*uring married life, part of the vocation is to lead your husband and children to heaven. God provides all the graces you need to do this. This is called sacramental grace, which comes only from receiving a sacrament. This special grace is God's direct help to you in fulfilling the duties of marriage.

*O*nce a person marries, they must be open to having children. However, some couples are not blessed with children. This is something God allows for a reason: perhaps they are called to adopt children, to be spiritual parents to others, or work in charities. Whatever they are called to, God gives them grace for their situation.

*I*f you are blessed with children, the duties of a mother include the taking care of both the spiritual and bodily needs of them. Mothers teach children their prayers, they teach them right from wrong, they show them a good example of a Catholic, they prepare them for the sacraments by teaching then their catechism, and they give them good food! Now you can see, again, why John Paul II wanted everyone to know how powerful women are when they are in love with Christ. They want to do these important and holy things for Him and His kingdom.

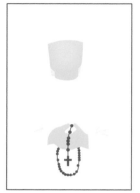

In days gone by, having a vocation to the consecrated life was considered to be an honor. Today, it is still an honor but many consecrated communities have all but disappeared. This is sad. Many girls grow up without having seen a sister (nun), let alone know one personally. However, this is a wonderful vocation and every girl should pray about it. It would seem that some religious orders are going to be seeing an increase in girls who have discerned this as a vocation and maybe one might be you! Ask God to help you know.

Consecrated life is a way of life where a girl, woman, chooses Jesus as her spouse. She freely agrees to live in community embracing the vows of poverty, chastity and obedience. After different stages, the woman will make her final vows, which means that she promises to live her entire life consecrated in this way.

There are many kinds of work the religious communities do. Here are some examples:

- *Contemplative orders are cloistered, which means the sisters don't leave their convent. Their lives are devoted to praying and making sacrifices for the entire world. Examples of these are the Poor Clares, Carmelites, and Perpetual Adoration nuns.*
- *Semi Contemplative orders do active work but usually don't leave their convents, except to work. They may teach or run orphanages. Examples of these sisters are Assumptive Sisters, Dominican Sisters of Our Lady Mother of the Eucharist, and Dominican Sisters of St. Cecelia.*
- *Active life communities dedicate their lives to teaching, hospital works, and mission work. They live and work outside a community house. Examples include Franciscan and Medical Missionaries of Mary.*

If someday you consider a vocation to the consecrated life, check out the orders that work in areas you like. Women cannot become priests, but they can influence many people by embracing consecrated life. Sisters have given many souls the love for the sacraments and the Faith through their work.

This is a kind of motherhood. It is called spiritual motherhood. All women are called to be mothers, but not all in the same way. If you don't have your own children, you can still be a mother through "mothering" children in hospitals, schools or in the mission field if you are a sister. Mother Teresa of Calcutta is a good example of being a spiritual mother. (Read about her story in this book.)

There are many ways to live the vocation of being single. This vocation is not the last choice of one who couldn't find a spouse. No, it is a calling just as special as marriage and consecrated life. All single people are called to the virtue of purity.

Single women have a job or career. They live and work in the world. Some take care of their elderly parents. In days gone by, girls would remain unmarried to care for priests. Pope Benedict XVI's sister, Maria, never married, worked as an administrative assistant and took care of the home for him. She was very happy and lived a full life.

There are women, also, who do not have a vocation to religious life or marriage but are called to be celibate for apostolic reasons. They may live with their families or wherever is convenient for professional reasons, or they may live together with other women in a home. Their vocation is to live and work in the world while also giving their lives to God. An example of this is Opus Dei.

Personality Plus!

Like Pope John Paul II said, women have special gifts and talents. Each person should use her gifts to get to heaven and to help others get there, too. Take this quiz to see what kind of personality you have. You might be a combination of two or three. Check the key below.

At a party, I like to:
a) Be the center of attention.
b) Plan everything and tell everyone what we're doing next.
c) I don't really like parties.
d) Go with the flow and have a good time.

At school there is a student counsel campaign. I would:
a) Be the one trying to get elected for social chairman.
b) Run for President!
c) Organize the campaign for a friend.
d) Figure I'd just wait and see what happens.

The group science project is due next week. I would:
a) Volunteer to design the artwork for the assignment.
b) Choose the topic and tell the other group members what they are to do.
c) Research the project and write a perfect report.
d) Take the part I was given and wait until the last minute to finish it.

At home with the family I like to:
a) Organize games and activities on the weekends for everyone.
b) Schedule the chores, meals and activities and supervise them all.
c) Read my books and work on my hobbies.
d) Do whatever my mom or sisters plans and just enjoy being home.

When friends come over:
a) We listen to music, dance and act silly.
b) I decide what we will do.
c) We work on hobbies or projects.
d) We do whatever comes up like going for a walk, watch a movie or bake cookies.

Personality Quiz Key

Mostly a's: You are a *Goodtime Gretchen*.

You are outgoing, love being around people, you like having fun and have a lot of creativity. These are awesome gifts to have while helping to spread the Faith. Why? Because you are a people magnet and everyone likes being around you. Just be careful not to let having fun take over your priorities.

Mostly b's: You are *Leslie the Leader*.

You are not afraid to take charge of anything. You can really use your talents to make a difference in the culture. Be sure you always make good choices because others will follow you. Take it easy though, you can easily dominate those who don't have as strong a personality as you do.

Mostly c's: You are *Organized Annie*.

You may not be belting out the orders but you are the person behind all the projects. You like to get good grades and work hard on the things you start. Your abilities can be used by God to further the Gospel. Sometimes though, you take things a little too seriously and need to chill.

Mostly d's: You are *Easygoing Elisa*.

Nothing really bothers you and you take things as them come. People like you because you are so easy to get along with. You can easily attract others to Jesus with such a likeable personality. However, be careful not to be so laid back that you go along with things that are wrong.

Isn't it nice to know that your faith supports women? How many examples of girls and women can you think of that have used their gifts to make a difference? Let's test your knowledge about different women in your faith history. Below, there are names of girl or women saints. Clues are under the names. See if you can match them up.

St. Helena 330 AD   *St. Flora 851 AD*   *St. Hunna 679 AD*

St. Olga 969 AD   *St. Julia 400 AD*   *St. Cecelia 177 AD*

St. Monica 337 AD

1. She is the mother of Constantine, emperor who legalized Christianity in the Roman Empire. She worked to convert him and he was baptized before his death. She is believed to have found the true cross of Jesus.

2. Mother of St. Augustine, she is known for perseverance in prayer. Her husband converted on his deathbed. Augustine converted after a sinful life and became a bishop and a great saint too!

3. She lived during the Roman persecution of Christians. She married a pagan and converted him. After being reported to the authorities, she refused to sacrifice to idols and was beheaded with a sword. She managed to live a short time because the executioner didn't sever her head completely. She is the patroness of musicians.

4. Married to a nobleman of France, she was generous and helpful to the poor and underprivileged. She was known as the "Holy Washerwoman" for doing menial tasks despite her social status.

5. A peasant who married Igor, Grand Duke of Russia. After her baptism she desired to convert her son and her country. Although she didn't accomplish this, her grandson Vladimir did because of her influence on him before her death.

6. Born a noble maiden, captured and sold into slavery, she was an excellent servant with a cheerful attitude. Her master considered her more valuable than all the possessions of a king. She was discovered to be a Christian, was tortured and crucified.

7. Born a Muslim, her mother secretly taught her the Catholic Faith. Her brother reported her to the authorities after their mother died. She was beaten and tortured. She later converted her brother and she died a martyr at the hands of the Muslims.

Answer Key:
1) St. Helena 2) St. Monica 3) St. Cecelia 4) St. Hunna 5) St. Olga 6) St. Julia 7) St. Flora

Great Women from 1000- 1900 AD

St. Teresa of Avila   Henriette Delille

Pauline Jaricot   Margaret Clitherow

St. Therese

1) She is known as the Little Flower. Born in France to a holy family, she entered the Carmelite Convent at an early age. She was humble and sweet and became a saint through the "little way," which was a way of achieving holiness by doing little things with love. She is

_____

2) She was African descent and born in New Orleans. She was a free Black woman during the years before the American Civil War. She gave up her life of ease and wealth for a life of poverty. She founded the Sisters of the Holy Family and endured ridicule, poverty and hard work. The sisters taught poor slave children, and performed other works of charity. At a time when there were no Black sisters, her achievements for God were monumental. She is

_____

3) She founded The Society for the Propagation of the Faith (an organization that contributes large amounts of money to foreign missions and is still in existence today!), Association of the Holy Childhood (an organization that collects money to build orphanages and schools in mission lands), and the Universal Living Rosary (an organization started in order to pray for those who have lost the Faith). Those jealous of her accused her of stealing money from these organizations. Two of her trusted business associates stole money from her charities, completely bankrupting her. She died in shame and poverty. She is

_____

4) She was the first woman to die during the persecution of Catholics in Protestant England. During this time, churches were burned, priests and nuns killed, and many faithful Catholics were thrown into prison to be executed later. She hid priests and held Mass in secret. Without her and others like her, the Catholic Church in England today would not exist. She is _____

5) She ran away to join the Carmelite Monastery. She was very ill. When she recovered, however, her legs were paralyzed for three years. Later she was cured. During her life she had many visions. She founded several convents and monasteries in Spain. She is

_____

Key: 1 is St. Therese; 2 is Henriette; 3 is Pauline; 4 is Margaret; 5 is St. Teresa of Avila

History is full of great, Catholic women, but what about more modern times? Are there any women who have recently made a difference in the world? Surely you can think of a couple of great women on your own, but just in case you need a little help check out the following stories and get inspired!

Dorothy Day

Dorothy Day, who lived from 1897-1980, is a story of a modern Mary Magdalene. Dorothy was raised mostly in Chicago by parents who had no religion and never went to church. As an adult, she considered herself an atheist and was involved with controversial issues of the day such as women's rights, birth control, and communism. On more than one occasion she was arrested for picketing. Dorothy had several immoral relationships with men and even had an abortion! After that she was married for a short time. Later she had a baby without being married.

Wow! What a life so far, huh? Well, Dorothy had a conversion to the Catholic faith and she and her daughter, Tamara Teresa were baptized. From then on, Dorothy's life was changed. She used her talents to help the poor and to do God's work. Dorothy co- founded a newspaper called The Catholic Worker, which spread the Catholic faith. She opened "Houses of Hospitality" in the slums where she fed the hungry, housed the homeless and clothed the naked. She worked tirelessly the rest of her life for peace and for the poor. Many other organizations were formed to care for the poor because of her example. Dorothy's diary reads…

> *"What we would like to do is change the world…we can work for the oasis, the little cell of joy and peace in a harried world."*

Dorothy believed that her efforts, the efforts of one person could make a difference in the world. What do you think? Do you think she's right? What can you do to make a difference?

Judie Brown

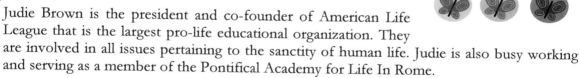

Judie Brown is the president and co-founder of American Life League that is the largest pro-life educational organization. They are involved in all issues pertaining to the sanctity of human life. Judie is also busy working and serving as a member of the Pontifical Academy for Life In Rome.

She has been on many televisions programs such at 20/20, 60 Minutes, Mother Angelica Live, The O'Reilly Factor, Good Morning America, Oprah, and Larry King Live. Her articles have been in newspapers and magazines across the country. Judie is also a regular guest on radio talk shows. She is fighting for the rights of the unborn, elderly and handicapped through educating people on the dignity of every human person.

Judie is married, has three children and nine grandchildren. Her main vocation is wife and mother. However, since 1969 she has worked in the pro-life movement, striving to make a difference in American culture. Judie's persistence and perseverance in writing and speaking is changing the culture of death in this country. Many people have changed their views because of her, especially the young generation.

Blessed Teresa of Calcutta

Blessed Teresa of Calcutta, known to most as Mother Teresa, was born Agnes Gonxha Bojaxhui on August 26, 1910 in Shkoder, Albania. She was eight years old when her father died. At 18, she left home to join the Sisters of Loreto as a missionary. She took the name Teresa after, St. Therese the Little Flower, the patroness of missionaries. She started out teaching in Calcutta, India at a girls' school.

On September 10, 1946, Teresa heard a call she described as "a call within the call." God had called her to leave the convent and help the poorest of the poor. With little money, a white habit with a blue stripe, and faith she went about helping the poor and dying. Soon, others joined her and her order of sisters started with 13 members. They were called Missionaries of Charity. With the help of Indian officials, she converted an abandoned Hindu Temple into a Home for the Dying. She wanted to give those who were dying a beautiful death.

One person can make a difference!

Mother Teresa also opened a hospice for those suffering from leprosy and an orphanage in Calcutta. But Mother's work didn't stop in India. Soon she had sisters in Venezuela, Asia, Africa, Europe and the United States all working for the poor, orphans, dying and those with AIDS. In 1963, she founded the Missionaries of Charity Brothers, Co-Workers of Mother Teresa, the Sick and Suffering Co-Workers, Lay Missionaries of Charity, and the Missionaries of Charity Fathers. Not bad for one little sister, huh?

At the time of her death, September 5, 1997, Mother Teresa had 4,000 sisters, 300 brothers, 100,000 lay volunteers, and 610 missions in 123 countries. She had also received numerous awards from many countries such as the Nobel Peace Prize.

Mother Angelica

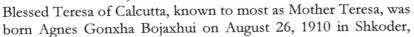

Rita Rizzo was born April 20, 1923 in Canton Ohio. She was the only child of a divorced couple. As a result of the divorce, Rita lived in poverty and was treated poorly by other Catholics and unfortunately by the sisters that taught her in school.

On August 15, 1944 Rita joined the Poor Clares in Cleveland, Ohio. At this time she experienced a freak accident while scrubbing the floor with an electric machine, leaving her with a serious spine injury. The pain was unbearable. After several treatments were tried, doctors decided to do surgery. Fearing the worst, Rita, now Sister Mary Angelica of the Annunciation, made a deal with God, saying, "if you allow me to walk again I will build a monastery for your glory and I will build it in the South!" Guess what!? Sister Angelica walked again, using braces, and she kept her promise.

Building takes money, right? Do you know how Sister Angelica raised the money to build the monastery in Irondale, Alabama? She made and sold fishing lures! Four other sisters and the now Mother Angelica headed to the south.

By 1976, Mother had written 50 booklets on the Catholic faith and had recorded 150 teaching tapes. She realized the impact of television on evangelization so when the opportunity came to record a teaching series for TV, Mother Angelica jumped at the chance. Soon she had a vision of building her own cable channel. In 1980 she converted a garage behind the monastery into a television studio. After many problems, Mother Angelica signed on her cable channel August 15, 1981 and named it Eternal Word Television Network (EWTN). This was aired via satellite, which is still going on today.

Are YOU ready to work for God?

Since then, Mother Angelica experienced a miracle healing of her back injury and was free of the braces she had been using. In 2001 she suffered health problems, especially a stroke and handed control of EWTN to a board of lay people. The stroke affected her speech and so she was forced to stop doing her famous show, Mother Angelica Live. Today she is living in the monastery and is the third oldest nun there. Many people have experienced conversions because of her satellite television studio. God used a little nun with a big faith, and no television experience to build a worldwide television network. Do you think one person can make a difference?

Vicki Thorn

Vicki Thorn started Project Rachel in Milwaukee, Wisconsin in 1984. She was one of the first ever to help women with post-abortion trauma. In the 1980's she was a young mother with a psychology degree who wanted to help friends she knew who were suffering after having an abortion. Today she has six children, is a trauma counselor, and a facilitator in bereavement loss and prenatal loss.

Project Rachel is a diocesan-based ministry that includes clergy with special training, spiritual directors, and therapists who help women and men who have been involved in abortion in any way. She wasn't expecting Project Rachel to grow outside her diocese, especially because the counseling profession denied that women and others were negatively affected by an abortion. Today she travels nationally and internationally speaking on post abortion trauma.

Think about it, we all make mistakes but think of a mistake that would change your life. Abortion is such a mistake. Not only does the baby suffer, but also anyone who is involved: the father, grandparents, bothers, sisters and friends. Women and men who are post-abortive have terrible guilt. Project Rachel helps them to heal and to forgive themselves.

The first thing Project Rachel does is put the person in touch with a priest who has had special training. There is such a burden lifted when the person can go to confession and know they are forgiven. So many women who have been helped by Project Rachel go on to understand the Church's teaching on abortion and even other teachings they rejected. Think of the impact this program has had on people! Vicki Thorn has trained between 4000-5000 clergy to aid in Project Rachel. Wow, one person can make a difference!

Other Examples of Modern Catholic Women:

Phyllis Schlafly

Phyllis Schlafly was born in St. Louis, Missouri. She attended Washington University and received her master's degree in political science in 1945 from Harvard University. In 1978 she earned a law degree and worked as a researcher for a number of Congressmen in Washington, D.C. She remained active in politics.

Phyllis is one of America's best known advocates for the dignity of the homemaker. She is the mother of six children and voted Illinois Mother of the Year in 1992. She was married for 44 years before her husband died and has 14 grandchildren. In a ten year battle starting in the 1970's, Phyllis campaigned against the Equal Rights Amendment. That's odd. Don't you think she would be for equal rights for women? Yes, she is for true equal rights, but she feared that this amendment would hurt women by forcing women to fight in combat and would lead to stuff like boy-girl bathrooms in public places. After all, we're all equal and equal means the same. Fortunately, all of her hard work paid off and the Equal Rights Amendment was defeated. She is a huge opponent of the feminist movement but a believer in true femininity (see the differences of feminism vs. femininity in this book.)

Phyllis Schlafly started an organization called Eagle Forum, which is a national organization of people who help in making public policy with offices in Washington, D.C.

She has authored several books, has a newsletter called The Phyllis Schlafly Report, writes for newspapers and magazines, does radio commentaries, and has appeared on television programs such as CBS Morning News, and CNN. You can learn more about Phyllis and what Eagle Forum is all about by going to www.eagleforum.org. Phyllis continues to be an advocate for women today.

Teresa Tomeo

Teresa is a very popular and well known Catholic radio and television personality. She started out in the news business after graduating from college in the beautiful state of Michigan. Teresa experienced many of the things that young girls experience today and she has graciously agreed to share some of her story and insights with the readers of "All Things Girl." Teresa learned a lot about the need to listen to God and obey His will for your life. Teresa shares her story in a book she wrote called, "Newsflash: My Surprising Journey from Secular Anchor to Media Evangelist."

Today Teresa speaks at many events along with doing her daily Catholic radio program called "Catholic Connection." Teresa encourages everyone to be whomever God has called them to be and with her own examples she shares how this can sometimes be difficult but is always rewarding!

Many hundreds of years ago there was a woman named Ruth. She was married to one of the sons of Naomi. Naomi was a Jewish woman who loved God so much that she made Ruth see how good it was to love God. Sadly, Naomi's sons died and so did Naomi's husband. This meant that Naomi only had two daughters-in-law left in her family. At that time Naomi was living in a land that was not her home. She was living in a place called Moab and Ruth was from Moab. Ruth was called a "Moabite."

What is so amazing about Ruth's story was that she was considered an "outsider." Because she didn't, at first, believe in the one true God, people didn't think of her as belonging to their crowd or culture. But remember that Naomi was a great witness to Ruth. This means that Naomi lived her life in such a way as people could look at her and sort of see a "walking bible."

Anyhow, once Naomi's sons died, Naomi encouraged her daughters-in-law to stay in their homeland of Moab but that she, herself, was going to return to her own homeland, Bethlehem. Naomi and her family had left Bethlehem because of a famine but now word was out that there was food in the land so she was going to go home.

Travelling back then was not like it is today. There were no planes to board and no busses or cars. Travel took weeks and months and was very difficult. So, when Naomi announced that she would go back to Bethlehem, it was quite surprising for Ruth to insist on going with her. Not only was it going to be a long and rough trip but Ruth really wouldn't be welcomed in Bethlehem because she was an outsider. But Ruth couldn't be deterred. That means she couldn't be held back from doing what she wanted to do which was stay with her mother-in-law, Naomi. This is what Ruth said to Naomi…

Do not ask me to abandon or forsake you! For wherever you go I will go, where you lodge I will lodge, your people shall be my people, and your God my God. Wherever you die I will die and there be buried. May the Lord do so and so to me, and more besides, if aught but death separates me from you!

Wow, those are pretty powerful words, aren't they? Can you imagine how Naomi must have witnessed to Ruth to make Ruth so in love with Naomi's God, your God? But the story gets even better.

Once Ruth and Naomi were back in Bethlehem, Ruth met a man named Boaz. He was a distant relative of Naomi's and looked upon Ruth with love. He wanted to marry her and when he made his intentions known all his friends and family gave him their blessings. This is what they said...

May the Lord make this wife come into your house like Rachel and Leah, who between them built up the house of Israel. May you do well and win fame in Bethlehem.

Ruth and Boaz's story is one of real true love and also the story of Jesus. Why? Because Ruth and Boaz had a son they named Obed. Obed then grew up and had a son named Jesse. Jesse is the father of David who became king and is the family tree in which Jesus Christ is born!

Family trees are so important and interesting. Make sure to work on yours by following the directions for making one in this book. Remember, you are a daughter of the King of Kings, Jesus! You are a precious jewel, a princess.

Feel like finding out more about some incredible women who lived even before Ruth? Check out some books on Rachel and Leah. See what you can find out about them that they would have been included in the blessing given to Boaz! Have fun and keep in mind that these are all your sisters-in-faith!

Everyday People

The stories above are inspiring aren't they? But, what about everyday people? Can one person really make a difference? Check out the true stories below and decide for yourselves.

Saved!

Several years ago Monica Cops was called by the local crisis pregnancy center. Being from Mexico, Monica was asked to go to the doctor with a young Hispanic woman who couldn't speak English so she could translate. She immediately called several friends to pray. The young woman was pregnant with her third child, homeless, unmarried, and abandoned by the father. She was considering an abortion. Monica took the young woman to a pro-life doctor where she had an ultrasound. At the end of the appointment, Monica begged the woman to give the baby life and to call Monica before any decisions were made. Monica never heard from the woman again.

A couple years later, on a cold and rainy March evening Molly Miller received a call. It was a woman calling from the Catholic bookstore where she had seen a poster advertising a conference. With a heavy Spanish accent the woman asked Molly some questions about the event since she and Monica were working on it. After this short conversation, the woman asked Molly if she could come and give her a ride home since it was cold and raining. Something very strong compelled Molly to go and pick up this woman who was a stranger.

That night Molly became friends with Bonny. Bonny told Molly that she was not married but had three children with two different fathers. One child was with her father and the other two were in foster care. She missed her children terribly and was working hard to get them back home. Over the next several months Bonny helped Molly with housework and they did things together for fun. Soon Bonny got two of her children back home.

One day Monica came for coffee at Molly's home at the time Bonny was doing some cleaning. Monica and Bonny met and had a brief discussion in Spanish. A couple weeks later, Monica realized that Bonny was the woman she had translated for several years before at the doctor's office. Bonny's third child was the child Monica had helped save from abortion.

Girls, always remember, that you can make a difference in your family, in your school and in your town. You don't have to be famous, super smart, gorgeous, or sensational in any way. Just living out your beliefs can and will cause this culture to change, one person at a time. If two little homemakers doing what they can in their own little corner of the world can make a difference, so can you. Rock on!

From Television to Radio and Beyond

Sally, a Catholic convert, was an anchorwoman for a television station in Omaha, Nebraska. After the birth of her first child she quit. She became a stay home mom and eventually had four more beautiful kids.

Molly Miller met Sally when their children attended the same Catholic school and the moms began carpooling. They became friends, sharing their struggles, prayers and some laughs along the way. It soon became apparent to Molly that Sally was not your ordinary mom. Using her gifts and experience in the media, Sally and her husband Mike, along with other folks, started a Catholic Radio station. Today, the radio station is thriving and Sally has moved on to work on other apostolates. She is active in her parish, and pro-life ministry. She is also pursuing a counseling degree.

You don't have to have the perfect life and the perfect circumstances or have it all together to live your life for God. He takes you wherever you are and walks along side you. Ordinary people can do extraordinary things, with God's help. Sally does it and so can you! Rock on!

Feminism vs. Femininity

History has shown that, yes, women have sometimes been cheated and degraded. Within the last 100 years in American history, women have fought for the right to vote and for the right to get paid the same as men for the same job. This was the start of the feminist movement. Sounds good, right? Well, women do deserve to be treated with dignity and respect, this is true. This is what God expected when He made man and woman equal but different.

However, did you know that feminists have a very different agenda than just the equal rights mentioned above? Again girls, ya gotta get the facts! You may be surprised. Check out the info below and see the contrast between feminism and femininity. Don't let yourself get caught up in the messages of feminism when they conflict with what God has in store for you! You don't need the heartache and confusion.

One of the most important things to remember about being a daughter of the King is that when He walked the earth, He made sure that women were treated as they were created: EQUAL. But equal just doesn't mean "the same." It means that God made everyone equal in dignity but with different gifts and so when girls try to be boys, or women try to be men, they are forgetting that God has great and wonderful things in store for everyone He made! Not just boys and not just girls!

This is so important to remember as you grow up. Keep talking with God so that He can help you be all He wants you to be and not what the world says you should be! Sometimes there's a big difference but only God's plan is the best for you!

Feminism vs. Femininity

Get the facts...Check out the chart...

Feminist Movement tells Women:	True Femininity tells Women:
X Motherhood takes away freedom from women.	Motherhood is a great gift. Women find great fulfillment and joy in having children or in being spiritual mothers.
X To be equal with men women have to be like men –dress like men, pursue a career, have an aggressive personality and refuse to be sensitive.	Women are equal in dignity to men but are different than men. The two compliment each other. Being sensitive, compassionate and gentle are gifts that women have and should embrace.
X Being a homemaker is a waste of intellectual talents. Only having a career is worthwhile.	By making a gift of herself as a homemaker and wife, women find happiness and fulfillment. It is the most worthwhile choice because of the influence a woman has on her family and through them, the world.
X Freedom is doing whatever you want without any rules.	Freedom is the ability to choose what is right and what is good.
X Women should be in control of their bodies. Birth control and abortion give you the freedom to pursue relationships without the burden of pregnancy.	Abortion and birth control hurt women and make them objects. Embracing life is a gift of self.
X Women have the right to be priests in the Catholic Church.	Just as a man will never be able to carry a baby within his body, women are not meant to be priests. This is God's plan

Celebrate Being a Girl!

What words describe the unique you?

Gentle
Creative
Intuitive
Compassionate
Nurturing
Sensitive
Caring
Generous
Intelligent
Detail Oriented
Giving

In days gone by, girls were educated in some different things than today. Homemaking and making pretty things were important. They were also cultured in music, language, art, and literature. Life wasn't all work though; girls played games and had fun too just like you. Going to and having parties were second nature to girls. Maybe you'd like to plan a party to just celebrate being a girl. What could you do? Hmmm, something different. Take a look at the activities in this book for you to do and see if your mom, sisters and friends would like to try them, too. Be sure to have plenty of snacks on hand.

Do you ever tell your mother you're bored? Well, here are some things girls did years ago for fun. Try them and see if they are just as fun today, in a world full of technology, as they were years ago. Chances are, you'll like these games too.

DUMB CRAMBO

There are two teams. Team 1 leaves the room to pick a word to act out and a word that rhymes with it to use as a clue. When Team 1 returns they will give Team 2 the clue and then act out the word. Team 2 guesses what the word is. Team 1 hisses loudly when the guesses are wrong. Team 2 will guess until they get the word. If they don't guess the word and they give up, Team 1 gets to go again. If Team 2 guesses correctly, they get to pick a word and act it out.

PINCH, NO SMILING

Everyone sits in a circle. Players are paired off. Each one of the pair pinches the nose, gently, please, of the other. The first to laugh or smile looses. All of the winners pair up and pinch the nose of the other. The first to laugh or smile looses. On it goes until there is a winner. This is a game of self-control and it is funny for others to watch.

TABOO

Players decide which letter of the alphabet will be forbidden, or Taboo. One person is chosen to be IT. Each player asks IT a question. IT has to answer the question without using the Taboo letter in the word. The questions go on until IT is forced to use the Taboo letter. Pick another IT and Taboo letter and continue the game until everyone has had a chance to be IT. Keep track of how many questions it takes before IT has to use the Taboo letter. Whichever IT had the most questions asked before using the Taboo letter is the winner.

PIÑATA, ONLY EASIER!

Who doesn't like candy and treats? Here's an easy and fun way to get them at your next party. Decorate a paper bag and fill it with candy and treats. Tie the bag shut and hang it from the ceiling or if the weather is nice, a tree outside. Blindfold one person, spin her around, give her a stick and see if she can hit the bag of candy. It's a good idea to allow each person only a couple of hits so that everyone gets a chance. Once the bag is hit and torn open, grab the candy!

FAMOUS ROMANCES

Each player has a heart with a name on it stuck to her back. The players do not know what the name is, but they do know it is part of a famous couple. Each person takes turns asking questions about the person on her heart. She has to keep asking questions until she guesses the name of the person on her heart. Famous couples could be Adam and Eve, Anthony and Cleopatra, Superman and Lois Lane, Mary and Joseph, Beauty and the Beast, Queen Isabella and King Ferdinand, and the list goes on and on.

Some girls have a shoe addiction, for others its lip gloss, still others it's purses! Here's a way to satisfy your craving for handbags-Make them yourself!

Purse-onality!

The "Absolutely You!" Handbag

Supplies: 19-by-6.5 inch piece of fake fur; Craft glue; Needle and Thread; Cording (long enough for the handle); 2 large fun buttons

Directions:

- Lay the fur down on a table, with the fuzzy part down. Measure 3 inches off one end.
- Apply craft glue to both sides –lengthwise-of the fabric, leaving the 3 inches at the end without any glue.
- Fold fur over all the way but the three inches on one end, and press edges firmly. These 3 inches will be the flap.
- Let your purse dry several hours before continuing.
- Sew the buttons to the back of the purse, one on each side of the flap. Be careful not to stitch through the front of the purse!
- Tie cord around buttons.

The "Extravagant Envelope" Purse

Supplies: Poly envelope with Velcro closure; Scissors; Ribbon; Hole punch; Sequences, trim, appliqués; Craft glue

Directions:

- Punch a hole on each side of the envelope, about 1 inch from the top, where the envelope opens.
- Make a strap for your purse out of ribbon, whatever length you like. Thread the ribbon through one of the holes, from the inside of the envelope out. Make a knot on the ribbon at the end that is inside the envelope. Take the other end of the ribbon and pass it through the other side hole, from the outside into the envelope, and again, tie a knot that will remain inside of the envelope.
- Now it's time to have fun decorating your purse with sequences, appliqués and trim using craft glue. Let it dry for several hours.

Expand Your Horizons

Some girls are "girlie girls"
and others "Tomboys."
Whatever your interests,
whatever your talents,
remember you are a girl,
you have the feminine genius!
There's nothing sadder than a girl
who wants to be a boy.
Do you know any girls like that?
Well, messages from the culture
can confuse girls on who they are
and what they ought to be.
You don't have to be someone
who likes frills
to embrace your feminine personality.
Girls can do so many things.
Expand your horizons and try new things.
You never know what kind of hidden talents
you may find!

Home-making Take a sewing class; Learn to embroider or cross-stitch; Plan a week's menu for your family; Learn to can homemade spaghetti sauce

Cultural Read a classic novel such as *Jane Eyre or Little Women*; Learn a language; Try a new dish from a different country; Learn about your heritage

Athletics Learn a new stroke in swimming; Take a tennis class; Take a golf lesson; Set up a game of croquet in your backyard

Hobbies Make a homemade movie; Grow kitchen herbs; Learn to play chess or card games; Take a pottery or mosaics class

Art/Music/Dance Listen to classical radio stations in the car; Take a painting / drawing class; Visit an art museum; Learn to play an instrument

Service Visit a nursing home; Serve at a soup kitchen; Volunteer at a hospital; Volunteer at parish activities such as picnics and dinners

Science and Technology Start a rock collection; Set up a bird feeder and watch birds; Learn a new computer program; Volunteer at the humane society

Start a Family Tree

This book has discussed a lot of influential women. I bet some of you have women in your own families that have done great things during their lives. Many people have discovered very cool stuff by doing a family tree. Below are some suggestions on how to get started. Here are some websites to check out once you get going: www.myheritage.com, www.ancestry.com, www.makemyfamilytree.com.

Whenever you start a project it's good to have a goal. For this project, the focus will be on finding out about the women in your family. Maybe you'll find photos, family recipes, letters, and even special family treasures such as a favorite book, rosary or game.

Some girls will just want to write things down in a journal. Others may want a journal plus a videotape of her talking with relatives and asking questions. Whatever way you want to do it, just do it!

Focus on one side of the family first otherwise it may be overwhelming. Start with the side of the family that has the oldest living relatives so you can talk to them personally. Decide from the start, how many generations you want to go back. This will keep you focused and give you a goal. Once you get started though, you may find you are going all the way back to the Mayflower!

Things You Will Need
Printable Family Tree Forms, check out the websites above; Index Cards and box; Journal or tablet for taking notes; Video camera; Binder or accordion folder; Photo albums

Facts, Just the Facts
When searching for your information, you need to know certain things:
- Full name of person you are researching including title (Miss, Ms., Mrs.)
- Spouse of person you are looking up including title
- Maiden names and wedding dates
- Birth dates and death dates
- Addresses or locations
- Baptismal and marriage certificates
- Military records if any

These are places to start. From there, ask questions of living relatives. Collect your information and put on index cards to lay out in order of the ancestors. Keep all your cards in a box. Any pictures you have keep in an accordion folder labeled properly. Organize your photos in a special album. Write stories you hear from your relatives in a journal. This is a hobby you can continue throughout your life. You'll be amazed about things you learn. Some families find that their great grandmother was a suffragette or a model. Others find wonderful love stories about an aunt an uncle.

Whatever you find, it will be an adventure!

Make a Time Capsule

Making a time capsule is fun for everyone. It's like preserving a piece of yourself. See the ideas below to start and then hey, be creative!

Start with a container. It can be big or small. Just be sure your things fit in it. Some ideas for a container are, plastic storage tub with a lid, a smaller plastic container such as Rubbermaid or Tupperware, an ice cream pail, or a 5 gallon drum with lid. Actually, anything that is plastic, metal or rubber will work. After you have chosen something as a container, feel free to decorate it.

There are many, many things you can put in your time capsule. The thing is, you want it to represent you, what things you like and what you believe in but also fun stuff that is popular right here and now. Here are some examples:

A state quarter; Any coin with the current year; The front page of your town newspaper for that day; A copy of your favorite magazine; A letter written by you to yourself to read in 10-20 years. You can explain what you want to be doing in the future, where you want to be living, and the things you think will be different in 10-20 years; Your favorite book; Movie or event ticket stubs; A picture of the current president; A piece of your artwork or something you've made such as a knitted scarf or an embroidered towel; Make a list or have pictures of your favorite movie stars; Souvenirs of your favorite vacation; Photos of family and friends with the date written on the back

Now that your capsule is full, what are you going to do with it? Well, a lot of people bury them. You can bury it in your backyard, maybe grandma's backyard, or at the family cabin. Make sure that your family owns the land, though. The capsule should be buried at least four feet under ground. If you choose to bury the capsule, you should seal the container with silicone to keep moisture out. If you don't want to bury your capsule, ask mom if you can store it in the attic or basement. Either way, label your container with directions and an opening date. Make sure you leave a note someplace safe to tell about the time capsule. It could be with your parents' important papers or in the family bible.

You can also make a specific time capsule say, for a special occasion such as your wedding day, your college graduation, or the day you go to the convent. Each of these special capsules would have specific things in them for that occasion. You may have collected special jewelry to wear on your wedding day, or you may write a letter to your future spouse. You may want to put a bottle of grape juice champagne in the capsule to celebrate your graduation, or a list of accomplishments you plan to do in your career. If you plan to join the convent you could have a hanky, your favorite prayer cards and a letter to Jesus.

Virtues to Live by...

What is a virtue? Very simply, a virtue is a good habit that inclines you to do whatever is good. Virtuous behavior helps you live a good, happy life. But there is more to virtues than that. A single good action does not constitute a virtue. For instance, a person wouldn't be considered to have the virtue of generosity if she shared her candy with her friends only once. In order to become a virtue, a good habit has to be repeated on a regular basis.

Perseverance

Perseverance is achieving the goal you have set for yourself in spite of difficulties such as tiredness, boredom, impatience and discouragement. It's the opposite of "throwing in the towel." Laziness is the opposite of perseverance. It's giving up when you get tired. It's changing your mind when you see the obstacles in your way.

Most people start projects with a lot of enthusiasm, but only a few people finish in the same way. Some don't even finish because they grow tired of what they are doing! Perseverance is finishing up what you started. It could be a board game ~even if you are losing~, sports, chores at home or reading a book from cover to cover before starting a new one. The typical words of a person that lacks perseverance is "I quit."

Perseverance is sticking to your commitments such as picking up your bedroom or volunteering at your parish picnic despite the hardships you may encounter such as low pay, being hot, or bored. Sometimes you may need to give up other more interesting activities in order to stick to your commitment. For instance, you promised your Grandma you would rake the leaves in her yard, but your friend Mindy asks you to go to a movie with her. You would honor your promise to Grandma if you chose to persevere.

Having a goal in mind is the key to perseverance. Once you have a goal, you make a plan to achieve it, and take account of the possible obstacles you may encounter. That way when they happen, you will be prepared to overcome them. What's the reason of having a goal in the first place? Well, it should be to give glory to God.

Here's a scenario: you have a science project due in a week. Your goal is to finish it before the weekend, so that you don't have to worry about it and you can enjoy time with family and friends. Great! What's the plan? Work on the project every day for an hour or so. What possible obstacles could you encounter? Friends calling on the phone, or maybe distractions from TV and computer could be a few. Once you are prepared, you will have no problem to saying "No" to obstacles. But remember, in order to achieve your goal, your real reason should be to glorify God. So, you tell God: *Lord, this science project is for You! I only want to do this to please You and to give You glory. Please help me not to get sidetracked. It's going to be hard, but I can do it with Your help.*

- Finish a project that you start before starting a new one.
- Use a calendar or planner so that you can see the kind of time you need to give things.
- Make a plan for every goal you want to achieve in your life.
  - Always remember that plans need to be evaluated, though, and that sometimes adjustments need to be made.
  - Ask mom or dad or grandma for advice when making long term goals or plans.
- Stick to your commitments, even if something more interesting to do comes up.
- Do everything to give glory to God, that way you won't want to leave things unfinished.
- Refuse to let laziness creep up on you when you are in the middle of a chore.
- Be positive: Remind yourself that you are a daughter of the King. You can do everything that God is calling you to do!

Things to Think About

an examination of conscience for girls

- Am I lazy?
- Do I finish what I started?
- Do I stick to my commitments?
- Do I set up goals for myself and make a plan to reach my goals?
- Am I a "quitter"?
- Do I realize that being a girl is very special?
- Do I use my feminine gifts such as compassion, intuition and gentleness to help others?
- Do I give myself generously to others?
- Do I pray to God for light to see clearly my vocation?
- Do I use the traits of my personality to make a difference in my family, school and parish?
- Do I buy into the feminist lies?

YOU'VE GOTTA HAVE A PLAN!

You know it is important to take care of and control your body. In the same way, you need to take care of your soul. You need to nourish it so that it can grow in friendship with Jesus. How is that done? You gotta have a plan!

Do you think athletes make it to the Olympics by chance? Do you think they go with the flow and train here and there and somehow one day they end up in the Olympic games winning a medal? Of course not, you know that! They have a plan that includes diet and training. They follow it everyday, even when they don't feel like it. This dedication allows the athlete to attain their goal, their dream of winning a medal at the Olympics.

Think about the purpose of your life, to know, love and serve God in this life and to be happy with Him forever in the next. Do you think you can achieve this goal without some planning and preparation?

Here's a simple but effective plan you can use your entire life to complete your training here and attain your Heavenly goal. You can also use the special "All Things Girl" journal to write your own plan, prayers, and thoughts.

Without me you can do nothing.
~John 15:5

WHAT THINGS SHOULD BE PART OF YOUR PLAN?

MORNING OFFERING:

A good way to start your day is to say, "Hello, Jesus!" The day ahead is a great gift from God. The morning offering consists of giving Jesus everything you will do and say that day. Tell Him you want to please Him and give Him glory in all that you do.

You can make up your own special prayer or you can choose one to memorize. For example, here's a very simple prayer.

"Good Morning dear Jesus this day is for you, I ask you to bless all that I say and do. Amen"

Or

"Oh Jesus through the Immaculate Heart of Mary I offer you the prayers, works, joys, and sufferings of this day, For all the intentions of Your Sacred Heart, in union with the Holy Sacrifice of the Mass said throughout the world today, in reparation for my sins, for the intentions of all our associates, and for the intentions of the Holy Father this month. Amen"

It is important to try and say your morning offering at the same time every day so that you remember to do it. Some girls will say it right when they wake up. Others, when they sit down to breakfast. Whatever works for you, just do it!

DAILY PRAYER.
Prayer is talking to Jesus. It is something great! Jesus prayed and openly encouraged his disciples to pray. And guess what? You, as a daughter of the King, are a disciple. How does a person learn to pray? Start out by setting aside 5 minutes of your day to sit down in a quiet place where there will be no distractions. Place yourself in the presence of Jesus, asking your guardian angel to help you start a conversation with Jesus. Because prayer is an intimate conversation with God, you can talk to God as your best friend and tell Him the things that are concerning you, what is making you happy, angry or sad; God is always listening. You may tell Him something like: *"Hi Jesus, guess what I'm doing today? I'm going to my cousins' house! Mom said I have to clean my room before going....and you know Jesus, I hate cleaning my room! But I guess I'll do it.... Maybe I should offer it up for a special intention, eh? Who needs prayers, Jesus?....."* On you go. You are praying! Slowly

increase the 5 minutes of prayer a day to 10 minutes. You will feel so happy when you spend time talking to Jesus every day!

THE ROSARY OF THE BLESSED MOTHER. Do you enjoy looking at family pictures and remembering those precious moments? Well, when you pray the rosary you contemplate moments in the lives of Jesus and Mary on each mystery. The rosary is divided into 4 parts: each part into five mysteries. For each mystery one Our Father and Ten Hail Mary's are prayed while you meditate on a certain time of Jesus' life. The name rosary means "crown of roses". Think about each of the Hail Mary's you pray as a rose offered to Our Lady. By the end of the rosary, you have offered her a huge bouquet of beautiful roses! If saying the entire rosary seems like a big task, start out with just one decade and slowly add one at a time. The idea is to make the effort and to keep on trying.

EXAMINATION OF CONSCIENCE AT NIGHT. Before going to bed, it's a good idea to take a quick look at your day in God's presence to see if you have behaved as a daughter of the King. An easy way to do this is by asking yourself these three questions:

- *What did I do today that was pleasing to God?*
- *What did I do today that was not pleasing to God?*
- *What does God want me to do better tomorrow?*

Ponder briefly on each question, and then follow with an act of contrition to tell Jesus that you are sorry for having offended Him. An Act of Contrition is just a short prayer telling Jesus you are sorry for your sins. It can be as simple as *"I'm sorry, Lord. Help me do better tomorrow."* Or it can be the traditional Act of Contrition, *" Oh my God, I am heartily sorry for having offended thee and I detest all my sins because of the loss of Heaven and the pains of Hell, But most of all because they offend Thee my God who are all good and deserving of all my love. I firmly resolve with the help of Thy grace, to confess my sins, to do penance and to amend my life, Amen."*

PRAY THREE HAIL MARY'S AT NIGHT BEFORE GOING TO BED ASKING THE BLESSED MOTHER TO HELP YOU KEEP YOUR HEART PURE.

Don't delay, start today, you can win the Olympics of the spiritual life!

A GIRL LIKE ME!

Saint Gianna
Beretta Molla

Gianna Beretta was born in Milan, Italy in 1922. She was the tenth of thirteen children who had a very happy childhood. She received an excellent Christian education from her parents, who always taught all their children that life is a marvelous gift from God.

As a teenager, Gianna was a good student and had many friends. She loved to go skiing and mountain climbing. She not only enjoyed having fun with her friends, but also she cared for their souls. This led her to join Catholic Action, a group for young people, where soon she became a leader and organized retreats, classes and helped the poor and needy of her town. One of Gianna's duties in Catholic Action was to pray every day for those who do not love Jesus. She kept her commitment very faithfully.

As Gianna grew into a young and beautiful woman, her desire to help people grew too. She had had an interest for medicine since she was young, so after finishing high school, Gianna decided to study to become a doctor, which she did in 1949. After obtaining her degree, she opened a medical clinic with her brother Fernando, who was also a doctor, in a neighbor town. Gianna loved children very much, and in 1952 she obtained an additional degree in pediatrics, which means a doctor for children.

Gianna had a great devotion to the Blessed Mother, and from an early age she had entrusted to Our Lady her whole life. In 1954, she went on a pilgrimage to Lourdes, France as a doctor, accompanying a train of sick people. During this trip, Gianna begged the Blessed Mother to help her discern what God wanted her to do with her life –her vocation-. She was not sure if God wanted her to be a missionary doctor, or to be married and have children. After this pilgrimage, God made her see clearly that He wanted Gianna to be married and have children. It was soon after that that she met her future husband, Pietro Molla. She reflected upon her vocation to be a wife, which she received and embraced as a gift from God.

Gianna and Pietro were married in 1955. They were both radiant with joy, happiness and enthusiasm to dedicate themselves to form a truly Christian family. After their marriage, three children were born: Pierluigi in 1956, Maria Zita in 1957 and Laura in 1959. During these years as a young wife and mother, Gianna continued her work as a doctor.

In 1961, she became pregnant again; this was her fourth child. Gianna was only two months pregnant when she became very ill and was rushed to the hospital. The tests revealed a very healthy baby, but also a life-threatening tumor growing in her uterus. The doctors gave her two options: To have an abortion, which would save her life but not the life of her baby; or a surgery to remove the tumor only, but this could bring further complications to her health. Wanting to save her baby's life, Gianna chose to have the surgery to remove the tumor, pleading to the doctors to save her child's life at all costs. She prayed very much for God's will to be done, placing her baby's life and hers in God's hands.

The surgery was successful in saving her baby's life, but the complications continued through her pregnancy. Gianna knew that God was going to ask her to sacrifice her life so that her child could live. She spent the seven remaining months of her pregnancy with an amazing peace of heart and unrelenting dedication to her tasks as wife, mother and doctor, always praying for God's will to be done.

A few days before her baby was due, Gianna expressed to her family: "If you must decide between me and the child, do not hesitate: choose the child. I insist on it. Save him". On the morning of April 21, 1962, her daughter Gianna Emanuela was born. That same day, Gianna's condition began to deteriorate; she was dying of an infection to the lining of the abdomen —a result of her choice to save her baby's life.

Gianna died a few days later. She was only 39 years old. During her last hours, amid unbearable pain, she kept repeating, "Jesus, I love you. Jesus, I love you." She could not receive Holy Communion because she was unable to swallow, so she begged the priest to place the Sacred Host at least on her lips, so that she could be as close to Jesus as possible.

Her husband Pietro has described Gianna's life as "an act and a perennial action of faith and charity; it was a non-stop search for the will of God for every decision and for every work, with prayer and meditation, Holy Mass and the Eucharist."

Gianna Beretta Molla was canonized on May 16th, 2004. It takes many centuries for many of the saints to be recognized by the Church for their heroic lives, but in Gianna's case, it only took four decades! Pope John Paul II said at Gianna's canonization that her witness was a hymn to life, and it was possible only after a life of preparation. Her husband Pietro, and three of her children were among the thousands of people that attended the Canonization ceremony in Rome.

Printed in the United States
136047LV00003B